INSTRUCTIONS

FOR

AMERICAN
SERVICEMEN

IN

BRITAIN
1942

ISBN 1-85124-085-3
©Bodleian Library, University of Oxford, 2004
All rights reserved
Designed and typeset by Dot Little
Printed by The University Press, Cambridge

British Library Cataloguing in Publication Data
A CIP record of this publication is available from the British Library

CONTENTS

FOREWORD

The original pamphlet, whose text is here reproduced, consists of seven pages of typescript, printed on poor quality foolscap size paper. It was issued by the United States War Department in 1942 and distributed to American servicemen who were going to Britain to prepare for the invasion of occupied Europe. Many of them had never been abroad before, and this pamphlet's avowed aim was to prepare these young American GIs for life in a very different country and to try and prevent any friction between them and the local populace. The Bodleian Library's copy was presented to it by the then Warden of Merton College, Sir John Miles, and is now held in Rhodes House, the dependent library of the Bodleian which is responsible for covering American history and politics.

The pamphlet attracted quite a lot of attention in Britain at the time, not least because it gave an unusually direct view of how the British were seen by others. An editorial in the London Times on July 14, 1942 suggested that it should become a best seller which "ought to be acquired by British readers in quantities unequalled even by the many works of Edgar Wallace or Nat Gould". Perhaps slightly tongue in cheek, the writer compared the pamphlet to the works of Irving, Emerson and Hawthorne, all writers who had tried to interpret Britain to an American audience, and commented that: "None of their august expositions has the spotlight directness of this revelation of plain common horse sense understanding of evident truths".

With remarkable succinctness, this pamphlet presents a 'snapshot' of wartime Britain, as seen by a sympathetic outsider. It has the same clarity and directness as the wartime newsreels and evokes the same response as Welcome to Britain, the famous film made by the Strand Film Company at the request of the Ministry of Information for showing to newly-arrived American servicemen. This too emphasises the British virtues of tolerance and fair play, shows Americans how to cope with everyday situations in the pub or on public transport (where for example blacks and whites might be sharing the same railway compartment, something outside the experience of many of those coming from the Deep South), and presents a picture of a people stoically coping with the problems caused by rationing or the blitz and quietly determined to see the war through to a victorious conclusion. This view of Britain may not have been the whole truth, but it was what people at the time wanted to believe and it has become firmly embedded in the folk memory of the Second World War ever since.

John Pinfold
Librarian, Rhodes House
1994

INSTRUCTIONS

FOR

AMERICAN SERVICEMEN

IN

BRITAIN

Issued by
War Department
Washington, D.C.

1942

—INTRODUCTION—

YOU are going to Great Britain as part of an Allied offensive—to meet Hitler and beat him on his own ground. For the time being you will be Britain's guest. The purpose of this guide is to start getting you acquainted with the British, their country, and their ways.

America and Britain are allies. Hitler knows that they are both powerful countries, tough and resourceful. He knows that they, with the other United Nations, mean his crushing defeat in the end.

So it is only common sense to understand that the first and major duty Hitler has given his propaganda chiefs is to separate Britain and America and spread distrust between them. If he can do that, his chance of winning *might* return.

NO TIME TO FIGHT OLD WARS. If you come from an Irish-American family, you may think of the English as persecutors of the Irish, or you may think of them as enemy Redcoats who fought against us in the American Revolution and the War of 1812. But there is no time today to fight old wars over again or bring up old grievances. We don't worry about which side our grandfathers fought on in the Civil War, because it doesn't mean anything now.

We can defeat Hitler's propaganda with a weapon of our own. Plain, common horse sense; understanding of evident truths.

The most evident truth of all is that in their major ways of life the British and American people are much alike. They speak the same language. They both believe in representative government, in freedom of worship, in freedom of speech. But each country has minor national characteristics which differ. It is by causing misunderstanding over these minor differences that Hitler hopes to make his propaganda effective.

BRITISH RESERVED, NOT UNFRIENDLY. You defeat enemy propaganda not by denying that these differences exist, but by admitting them openly and then trying to understand them. For instance: The British are often more reserved in conduct than we. On a small crowded island where forty-five million people live, each man learns to guard his privacy carefully—and is equally careful not to invade another man's privacy.

So if Britons sit in trains or busses without striking up conversation with you, it doesn't mean they are being haughty and unfriendly. Probably they are paying more attention to you than you think. But they don't speak to you because they don't want to appear intrusive or rude.

Another difference. The British have phrases and colloquialisms of their own that may sound funny to you. You can make just as many boners in their eyes. It isn't a good idea, for instance, to say "bloody" in mixed company in Britain—it is one of their worst swear words. To say "I look like a bum" is offensive to their ears, for to the British this means that you look like your own backside. It isn't important—just a tip if you are trying to shine in polite society. Near the end of this guide you will find more of these differences of speech.

British money is in pounds, shillings, and pence. (This also is explained more fully later on.) The British are used to this system and they like it, and all your arguments that the American decimal system is better won't convince them. They won't be pleased to hear you call it "funny money", either. They sweat hard to get it (wages are much lower in Britain than America) and they won't think you smart or funny for mocking at it.

DON'T BE A SHOW OFF. The British dislike bragging and showing off. American wages and American soldier's pay are the highest in the world. When pay day comes it would be sound practice to learn to spend your money according to British standards. They consider you highly paid. They won't think any better of you for throwing money around; they are more likely to feel that you haven't learned the common-sense virtues of thrift. The British "Tommy" is apt to be specially touchy about the difference between his wages and yours. Keep this in mind. Use common sense and don't rub him the wrong way.

You will find many things in Britain physically different from similar things in America. But there are also important similarities——our common speech, our common law, and our ideals of religious freedom were all brought from Britain when the Pilgrims landed at Plymouth Rock. Our ideas about political liberties are also British and parts of our own Bill of Rights were borrowed from the great chapters of British liberty.

Remember that in America you like people to conduct themselves as we do, and to respect the same things. Try to do the same for the British and respect the things they treasure.

THE BRITISH ARE TOUGH. Don't be misled by the British tendency to be soft-spoken and polite. If they need to be, they can be plenty tough. The English language didn't spread across the oceans and over the mountains and jungles and swamps of the world because these people were panty-waists.

Sixty thousand British civilians—men, women, and children—have died under bombs, and yet the morale of the British is unbreakable and high. A nation doesn't come through that, if it doesn't have plain, common guts. The British are tough, strong people, and good allies.

You won't be able to tell the British much about "taking it." They are not particularly interested in taking it any more. They are far more interested in getting together in solid friendship with us, so that we can all start dishing it out to Hitler.

YOU will find out right away that England is a small country, smaller than North Carolina or Iowa. The whole of Great Britain—that is England and Scotland and Wales together—is hardly bigger than Minnesota. England's largest river, the Thames (pronounced "Tems") is not even as big as the Mississippi when it leaves Minnesota. No part of England is more than one hundred miles from the Sea.

If you are from Boston or Seattle the weather may remind you of home. If you are from Arizona or North Dakota you will find it a little hard to get used to. At first you will probably not like the almost continual rains and mists and the absence of snow and crisp cold. Actually, the city of London has less rain for the whole year than many places in the United States, but the rain falls in frequent drizzles. Most people get used to the English climate eventually.

If you have a chance to travel about you will agree that no area of the same size in the United States has such a variety of scenery. At one end of the English channel there is coast like that of Maine. At the other end are the great white chalk cliffs of Dover. The lands of South England and the Thames Valley are like farm or grazing lands of the eastern United States, while the lake country in the north of England and the highlands of Scotland are like the White Mountains of New Hampshire. In the east, where England bulges out toward Holland, the land is almost Dutch in appearance, low, flat, and marshy. The great wild moors of Yorkshire in the north and Devon in the southwest will remind you of the Badlands of Dakota and Montana.

AGE INSTEAD OF SIZE. On furlough you will probably go to the cities, where you will meet the Briton's pride in age and tradition. You will find that the British care little about size, not having the "biggest" of many things as we do. For instance, London has no skyscrapers. Not because English architects couldn't design one, but because London is built on swampy ground, not on a rock like New York and skyscrapers need something solid to rest their foundations on. In London they will point out to you buildings like Westminster Abbey, where England's kings and greatest men are buried, and St. Paul's Cathedral with its famous dome, and the Tower of London, which was built almost a thousand years ago. All of these buildings have played an important part in England's history. They mean just as much to the British as Mount Vernon or Lincoln's birthplace do to us.

The largest English cities are all located in the lowlands near the various seacoasts. In the southeast, on the Thames, is London—which is the combined New York, Washington, and Chicago not only of England but of the far-flung British Empire. Greater London's huge population of twelve million people is the size of Greater New York City and all its suburbs with the nearby New Jersey cities thrown in. It is also more than a quarter of the total population of the British Isles. The great "midland" manufacturing cities of Brimingham, Sheffield, and Coventry (sometimes called "the Detroit of Britain") are located in the central part of England. Nearby on the west coast are the textile and shipping centers of Manchester and Liverpool. Further north, in Scotland, is the world's leading shipbuilding center of Glasgow. On the east side of Scotland is the historic Scottish capital, Edinburgh, scene of the tales of Scott and Robert Louis Stevenson which many of you read in school. In southwest England at the broad mouth of the Severn is the great port of Bristol.

REMEMBER THERE'S A WAR ON. Britain may look a little shop-worn and grimy to you. The British people are anxious to have you know that you are not seeing their country at its best. There's been a war on since 1939. The houses haven't been painted because factories are not making paint—they're making planes. The famous English gardens and parks are either unkept because there are no men to take care of them, or they are being used to grow needed vegetables. British taxicabs look antique because Britain makes tanks for herself and Russia and hasn't time to make new cars. British trains are cold because power is needed for industry, not for heating. There are no luxury dining cars on trains because total war effort has no place for such frills. The trains are un-washed and grimy because men and women are needed for more important work than car-washing. The British people are anxious for you to know that in normal times Britain looks much prettier, cleaner, neater.

BRITAIN THE CRADLE OF DEMOCRACY. Although you'll read in the papers about "lords" and "sirs", England is still one of the great democracies and the cradle of many American liberties. Personal rule by the King has been dead in England for nearly a thousand years. Today the King reigns, but does not govern. The British people have great affection for their monarch but they have stripped him of practically all political power.

It is well to remember this in your comings and goings about England. Be careful not to criticize the King. The British feel about that the way you would feel if anyone spoke against our country or our flag. Today's King and Queen stuck with the people through the blitzes and had their home bombed just like anyone else, and the people are proud of them.

Today the old power of the King has been shifted to Parliament, the Prime Minister, and his Cabinet. The British Parliament has been called the mother of parliaments, because almost all the representative bodies in the world have been copied from it. It is made up of two houses, the House of Commons and the House of Lords. The House of Commons is the most powerful and is elected by all adult men and women in the country, much like our Congress. Today the House of Lords can do little more than add its approval to laws passed by the House of Commons. Many of the "titles" held in the lords (such as "baron" and "duke" and "earl") have been passed from father to son for hundreds of years. Others are granted in reward for outstanding achievement, much as American colleges and universities give honorary degrees to famous men and women. These customs may seem strange and old-fashioned but they give the British the same feeling of security and comfort that many of us get from the familiar ritual of a church service.

The important thing to remember is that within this apparently old-fashioned framework the British enjoy a practical, working twentieth century democracy which is in some ways even more flexible and sensitive to the will of the people than our own.

—THE PEOPLE—THEIR CUSTOMS AND MANNERS—

THE BEST WAY to get on in Britain is very much the same as the best way to get on in America. The same sort of courtesy and decency and friendliness that go over big in America will go over big in Britain. The British have seen a good many Americans and they like Americans. They will like your frankness as long as it is friendly. They will expect you to be generous. They are not given to back-slapping and they are shy about showing their affections. But once they get to like you they make the best friends in the world.

In "getting along" the first important thing to remember is that the British are like the Americans in many ways—but not in all ways. You will quickly discover differences that seem confusing and even wrong. Like driving on the left side of the road, and having money based on an "impossible" accounting system, and drinking warm beer. But once you get used to things like that, you will realize that they belong to England just as baseball and jazz and coca-cola belong to us.

THE BRITISH LIKE SPORTS. The British of all classes are enthusiastic about sports, both as amateurs and as spectators of professional sports. They love to shoot, they love to play games, they ride horses and bet on horse races, they fish. (But be careful where you hunt or fish. Fishing and hunting rights are often private property). The great "spectator" sports are football in the autumn and winter and cricket in the spring and summer. See a "match" in either of these sports whenever you get a chance. You will get a kick out of it—if only for the differences from American sports.

Cricket will strike you as slow compared with American baseball, but it isn't easy to play well. You will probably get more fun out of "village cricket" which corresponds to sandlot baseball than you would out of the big three-day professional matches. The big professional matches are often nothing but a private contest between the bowler (who corresponds to our pitcher) and the batsman (batter) and you have to know the fine points of the game to understand what is going on.

Football in Britain takes two forms. They play soccer, which is known in America; and they also play "rugger", which is a rougher game and closer to American football, but is played without the padded suits and headguards we use. Rugger requires fifteen on a side, uses a ball slightly bigger than our football, and allows a lateral but not forward passing. The English do not handle the ball as cleanly as we do, but they are far more expert with their feet. As in all English games, no substitutes are allowed. If a man if injured, his side continues with fourteen players and so on.

You will find that English crowds at football or cricket matches are more orderly and polite to the players than American crowds. If a fielder misses a catch at cricket, the crowd will probably take a sympathetic attitude. They will shout "good try" even if it looks to you like a bad fumble. In America the crowd would probably shout "take him out". This contrast should be remembered. It means that you must be careful in the excitement of an English game not to shout out remarks which everyone in America would understand, but which the British might think insulting.

In general more people play games in Britain than in America and they play the game even if they are not good at it. You can always find people who play no better than you and are glad to play with you. They are good sportsmen and are quick to recognize good sportsmanship wherever they meet it.

INDOOR AMUSEMENTS. The British have theaters and movies (which they call "cinemas") as we do. But the great place of recreation is the "pub." A pub, or public house, is what we could call a bar or tavern. The usual drink is beer, which is not an imitation of German beer as our beer is, but ale. (But they usually call it beer or "bitter.") Not much whiskey is now being drunk. Wartime taxes have shot the price of a bottle up to about $4.50. The British are beer-drinkers—and can hold it. The beer is now below peacetime strength, but can still make a man's tongue wag at both ends.

You will be welcome in the British pubs as long as you remember one thing. The pub is "the poor man's club," the neighborhood or village gathering place, where the men have come to see their friends, not strangers. If you want to join a darts game, let them ask you first (as they probably will). And if you are beaten it is the custom to stand aside and let someone else play.

The British make much of Sunday. All the shops are closed, most of the restaurants are closed, and in the small towns there is not much to do. You had better follow the example of the British and try to spend Sunday afternoon in the country.

British churches, particularly the little village churches, are often very beautiful inside and out. Most of them are always open and if you feel like it, do not hesitate to walk in. But do not walk around if a service is going on.

You will naturally be interested in getting to know your opposite number, the British soldier, the "Tommy" you have heard and read about. You can understand that two actions on your part will slow up the friendship—swiping his girl, and not appreciating what his army has been up against. Yes, and rubbing it in that you are better paid than he is.

Children the world over are easy to get along with. British children are much like our own. The British have reserved much of the food that gets through solely for their children. To the British children you as an American will be "something special." For they have been fed at their schools and impressed with the fact that the food they ate was sent to them by Uncle Sam. You don't have to tell the British about lend-lease food. They know about it and appreciate it.

KEEP OUT OF ARGUMENTS. You can rub a Britisher the wrong way by telling him "we came over and won the last one." Each nation did its share. But Britain remembers that nearly a million of her best manhood died in the last war. America lost 60,000 in action.

Such arguments and the war debts along with them are dead issues. Nazi propaganda now is pounding away day and night asking the British people why they should fight "to save Uncle Shylock and his silver dollar." Don't play into Hitler's hands by mentioning war debts.

Neither do the British need to be told that their armies lost the first couple of rounds in the present war. We've lost a couple, ourselves, so do not start off by being critical of them and saying what the Yanks are going to do. Use your head before you sound off, and remember how long the British alone held Hitler off without any help from anyone.

In the pubs you will hear a lot of Britons openly criticizing their government and the conduct of the war. That isn't an occasion for you to put in your two-cents worth. It's their business, not yours. You sometimes criticize members of your own family—but just let an outsider start doing the same, and you know how you feel!

The Briton is just as outspoken and independent as we are. But don't get him wrong. He is also the most lawabiding citizen in the world, because the British system of justice is just about the best there is. There are fewer murders, robberies, and burglaries in the whole of Great Britain in a year than in a single large American city.

Once again, look, listen, and learn before you start telling the British how much better we do things. They will be interested to hear about life in America and you have a great chance to overcome the picture many of them have gotten from the movies of an America made up of wild Indians and gangsters. When you find differences between British and American ways of doing things, there is usually a good reason for them.

British railways have dinky freight cars (which they call "goods wagons") not because they don't know any better. Small cars allow quicker handling of freight at the thousands and thousands of small stations.

British automobiles are little and low-powered. That's because all the gasoline has to be imported over thousands of miles of ocean.

Brtish taxicabs have comic-looking front wheel structures. Watch them turn around in a 12-foot street and you'll understand why.

The British don't know how to make a good cup of coffee. You don't know how to make a good cup of tea. It's an even swap.

The British are leisurely—but not really slow. Their crack trains hold world speed records. A British ship held the trans-Atlantic record. A British car and a British driver set world's speed records in America.

Do not be offended if Britishers do not pay as full respects to national or regimental colors as Americans do. The British do not treat the flag as such an important symbol as we do. But they pay more frequent respect to their national anthem. In peace or war "God Save the King" (to the same tune of our "America") is played at the conclusion of all public gatherings such as theater performances. The British consider it bad form not to stand at attention, even if it means missing the last bus. If you are in a hurry, leave before the national anthem is played. That's considered alright.

On the whole, British people—whether English, Scottish, or Welsh—are open and honest. If you are on furlough and puzzled about directions, money, or customs, most people will be anxious to help you as long as you speak first and without bluster. The best authority on all problems is the nearest "bobby" (policeman) in his steel helmet. British police are proud of being able to answer almost any question under the sun. They're not in a hurry and they'll take plenty of time to talk to you.

The British will welcome you as friends and allies. But remember that crossing the ocean doesn't automatically make you a hero. There are housewives in aprons and youngsters in knee pants in Britain who have lived through more high explosives in air raids than many soldiers saw in first class barrages in the last war.

AT HOME in America you were in a country at war. Since your ship left port, however, you have been in a *war zone*. You will find that all Britain is a war zone and has been since September 1939. All this has meant great changes in the British way of life.

Every light in England is blacked out every night and all night. Every highway signpost has come down and barrage balloons have gone up. Grazing land is now ploughed for wheat and flower beds turned into vegetable gardens. Britain's peacetime army of a couple of hundred thousand has been expanded to over two million men. Everything from the biggest factory to the smallest village workshop is turning out something for the war, so that Britain can supply arms for herself, for Libya, India, Russia, and every front. Hundreds of thousands of women have gone to work in factories or joined the many military auxiliary forces. Old-time social distinctions are being forgotten as the sons of factory workers rise to be officers in the forces and the daughters of noblemen get jobs in munitions factories.

But more important than this is the effect of the war itself. The British have been bombed, night after night and month after month. Thousands of them have lost their houses, their possessions, their families. Gasoline, clothes, and railroad travel are hard to come by and incomes are cut by taxes to an extent we Americans have not even approached. One of the things the English always had enough of in the past was soap. Now it is so scarce that girls working in the factories often cannot get the grease off their hands or out of their hair. And food is more strictly rationed than anything else.

THE BRITISH CAME THROUGH. For many months the people of Britain have been doing without things which Americans take for granted. But you will find that shortages, discomforts, blackouts, and bombings have not made the British depressed. They have a new cheerfulness and a new determination born out of hard times and tough luck. After going through what they have been through it's only human nature that they should be more than ever determined to win.

You are coming to Britain from a country where your home is still safe, food is still plentiful, and lights are still burning. So it is doubly important for you to remember that the British soldiers and civilians have been living under a tremendous strain. It is always im-polite to criticize your hosts. It is militarily stupid to insult your allies. So stop and think before you sound off about lukewarm beer, or cold boiled potatoes, or the way English cigarettes taste.

If British civilians look dowdy and badly dressed, it is not because they do not like good clothes or know how to wear them. All clothing is rationed and the British know that they help war production by wearing an old suit or dress until it cannot be patched any longer. Old clothes are "good form."

One thing to be careful about—if you are invited into a British home and the host exhorts you to "eat up there's plenty on the table," go easy. It may be the family's rations for a whole week spread out to show their hospitality.

WASTE MEANS LIVES. It is always said that Americans throw more food into their garbage cans than any other country eats. It is true. We have always been a "producer" nation. Most British food is imported even in peacetimes, and for the last two years the British have been taught not to waste the things that their ships bring in from abroad. British seamen die getting those convoys through. The British have been taught this so thoroughly that they now know that gasoline and food represent the lives of merchant sailors. And when you burn gasoline needlessly, it will seem to them as if you are wasting the blood of those seamen—when you destroy or waste food you have wasted the life of another sailor.

BRITISH WOMEN AT WAR. A British woman officer or non-commissioned officer can—and often does—give orders to a man private. The men obey smartly and know it is no shame. For British women have proven themselves in this way. They have stuck to their posts near burning ammunition dumps, delivered messages afoot after their motorcycles have been blasted from under them. They have pulled aviators from burning planes. They have died at the gun posts and as they fell another girl has stepped directly into the position and "carried on." There is not a single record in this war of any British woman in uniformed service quitting her post or failing in her duty under fire.

Now you understand why British soldiers respect the women in uniform. They have won the right to the utmost respect. When you see a girl in khaki or air-force blue with a bit of ribbon on her tunic—remember she didn't get it for knitting more socks than anyone else in Ipswich.

ALMOST before you meet the people you will hear them speaking "English." At first you may not understand what they are talking about and they may not understand what you say. The accent will be different from what you are used to, and many of the words will be strange, or apparently wrongly used. But you will get used to it. Remember that back in Washington stenographers from the South are having a hard time to understand dictation given by business executives from New England and the other way around.

In England the "upper crust" speak pretty much alike. You will hear the news broadcaster for the BBC (British Broadcasting Corporation). He is a good example, because he has been trained to talk with the "cultured" accent. He will drop the letter "r" (as people do in some sections of our own country) and will say "hyah" instead of "here." He will use the broad a pronouncing all the a's in "Banana" like the a in "father." However funny you may think this is, you will be able to understand people who talk this way and they will be able to understand you. And you will soon get over thinking it is funny.

You will have more difficulty with some of the local dialects. It may comfort you to know that a farmer or villager from Cornwall very often can't understand a farmer or villager in Yorkshire or Lancashire. But you will learn—and they will learn—to understand you.

SOME HINTS ON BRITISH WORDS. British slang is something you will have to pick up for yourself. But even apart from slang, there are many words which have different meanings from the way we use them and many common objects have different names. For instance, instead of railroads, automobiles, and radios, the British will talk about railways, motorcars, and wireless sets. A railroad tie is a sleeper. A freight car is a goods wagon. A man who works on the roadbed is a navvy. A streetcar is a tram. Automobile lingo is just as different. A light truck is a lorry. The top of a car is the hood. What we call the hood (of the engine) is a bonnet. The fenders are wings. A wrench is a spanner. Gas is petrol—if there is any.

Your first furlough may find you in some small difficulties because of language difference. You will have to ask for sock suspenders to get garters and for braces instead of suspenders—if you need any. If you are standing in line to buy (book) a railroad ticket or a seat at the movies (cinema) you will be queuing (pronounced "cueing") up before the booking office. If you want a beer quickly, you had better ask for the nearest pub.

You will get your drugs at a chemist's and your tobacco at a tobacconist, hardware at an ironmonger's. If you are asked to visit somebody's apartment, he or she will call it a flat.

A unit of money, not shown in the following table, which you will sometimes see advertised in the better stores is the guinea (pronounced "ginny" with the "g" hard as in "go"). It is worth 21 shillings, or one pound plus one shilling. There is no actual coin or bill of this value in use. It is merely a quotation of price.

A coin not shown in the table below is the gold sovereign, with a value of one pound. You will read about it in English literature but you will probably never see one and need not bother about it.

WEIGHTS AND MEASURES: The measures of length and weight are almost the same as those used in America. The British have inches, feet, yards, pints, quarts, gallons, and so forth. You should remember, however, that the English (or "Imperial") gallon contains about one-fifth more liquid than the American gallon.

—SOME IMPORTANT DO'S AND DON'TS—

BE FRIENDLY—but don't intrude anywhere it seems you are not wanted.

You will find the British money system easier than you think. A little study beforehand on shipboard will make it still easier.

You are higher paid than the British "Tommy." Don't rub it in. Play fair with him. He can be a pal in need.

Don't show off or brag or bluster—"swank" as the British say. If somebody looks in your direction and says, "He's chucking his weight about," you can be pretty sure you're off base. That's the time to pull in your ears.

If you are invited to eat with a family don't eat too much. Otherwise you may eat up their weekly rations.

Don't make fun of British speech or accents. You sound just as funny to them but they will be too polite to show it.

Avoid comments on the British Government or politics.

Don't try to tell the British that America won the last war or make wise-cracks about the war debts or about British defeats in this war.

NEVER criticize the King or Queen.

Don't criticize the food, beer, or cigarettes to the British. Remember they have been at war since 1939.

Use common sense on all occasions. By your conduct you have great power to bring about a better understanding between the two countries after the war is over.

You will soon find yourself among a kindly, quiet, hard-working people who have been living under a strain such as few people in the world have ever known. In your dealings with them, let this be your slogan:

It is always impolite to criticize your hosts;
it is militarily stupid to criticize your allies.

TABLE OF BRITISH CURRENCY

Symbol	Name	British value	American value (approximate)
Copper Coins			
¼d.	farthing (rare)	¼ penny	½ cent
½d.	halfpenny ("hay-p'ny")	½ penny	1 cent
1d.	penny	1 penny	2 cents
3d.	threepence ("thruppence" or "thrup'ny bit"; rare)	3 pence	5 cents
Silver Coins			
3d.	threepence ("thruppence" or "thrup'ny bit"; not common in cities)	3 pence	5 cents
6d.	sixpence	6 pence	10 cents
1s.	shilling (or "bob")	12 pence	20 cents
2s.	florin (fairly rare)	2 shillings	40 cents
2s. 6d.	half crown (or "two and six")	2 shillings	50 cents
5s.	crown (rare)	5 shillings	$1.00
Paper Currency			
10s.	10-shilling note	10 shillings (or ½ pound)	$2.00
£1	pound note	20 shillings	$4.00
£5	5-pound note	5 pounds	$20.00